Sophie Modert

The Colours of Benin

Textes et photos : © *2017 Sophie Modert*
Mise en page et illustration de couverture : © *2017 Tom Weber*

Edition : BoD - Books on Demand
12/14 rond-point des Champs Elysées
75008 Paris
Imprimé par BoD – Books on Demand, Norderstedt
ISBN : 978-2-3221-5724-2
Dépôt légal : **Mai 2017**

"When you leave Africa, as the plane lifts, you feel that you are leaving more than a continent, you're leaving a state of mind. Whatever awaits you at the other end of your journey will be a different order of existence."

- Francesca Marciano

For my sister Catherine, who encouraged me to go on this journey and without whom I might never had completed it.

The colours of Benin

A dusty road painted in red,

Framed by tradesmen and shops

Containing simple and pure joy of life,

Just as kindness and familiarity.

Laughing is thrown into the air

And you feel embraced

By human warmth and generosity,

Lingering around all the way.

They are wrapped into friendly words,

A smile or curious looks,

Gifts given to strangers

As well as to family and friends,

Which surpass the value

Of the material goods

That are ready to be sold.

The colourful clothes

Taking part in the scenery

Translate the essence of this world

To the stranger's admiring eye,

Who is no longer blinded

By the grey veil

Created by the western world.

Échos musicaux

Une famille accueillante

Qui inclut tout un pays,

Et danse à une chanson

Joyeuse et chaleureuse,

Peinte par les couleurs

De la chaleur humaine,

Dont le rythme réunit

Les mamans et les papas,

Les fofos et les dadas

De cette grande famille

Qui embrasse la mélodie

De la vie.

Une chanson dont les échos

Évoquent des rois et des palais,

Des artisans et des traditions,

Dessinant le portrait

D'un passé glorieux,

Dont les couleurs échappent

À la conception artistique

Du monde moderne.

Fofo=Frère en langue Fon, la langue la plus parlée du Bénin
Dada=Soeur en langue Fon

A concert of languages

Sweet innocent smiles,

Embraced by human warmth,

Are dancing with tender words,

Relieving them from

Their material pall,

The grey veil

Of differently coloured languages

And revealing

Their immaterial substance,

A composition of all colours.

A music written

In a universal language,

Playing in the air

And captured

By the curious gaze

Of listening children.

Bonjour Dada!

Nfongangia mes amis !

Colonization

Written down in history

In a deep black ink,

But covered in dust

In an anthology

Of the crimes against humanity,

Committed by humanity,

It is lying in a corner

In the attic of history,

Willingly neglected by those

Who bear responsibility,

So the story will not be rewritten

In the ink of culpability.

An evil still living

Silently among us,

Its footprints only visible

In the sands of Ouidah,

Where they cannot be washed away.

A place of remembrance,

Cultural and religious identity,

Celebrating the very reasons

For the composition

Of this chapter of history

And still making them rise.

The gate of no return in Ouidah, where many slaves from western Africa were sold, tortured and deported. It is the only important memorial of slavery in Benin.
But Ouidah is also of essential importance to the cult of Vodoo, with many celebrations held at the beach every year, in front of the gate of no return.

Cultural self-doubts

The collective mind

Is still dancing

To the melody of imperialism,

Its colours painting

A feeling of inferiority

And admiration for dancers

Of differently coloured songs.

Their notes are playing

Above the streets,

Portraying an illusionary reality

And transforming

The colour of innocence

Into the colour

Of superiority and perfection.

A song of promises,

Indicating a dance technique

That is believed necessary

To be a wholesome member

Of the global dance floor.

"Is it rare to have contact with white people?"

"It is and I've already been told that I'm very lucky to be friends with you. Do you want to know why I don't have a girlfriend?"

"Why?"

"Because I want a foreign girlfriend and I would consider it as a great honour to have a mixed child in my family."

Artistic collaboration

"God can do anything!"

An imported religion,

That has revealed itself

As an essential brushstroke

To the contours of society's portrait,

But clothed in the colours

Of the artistic creation

Of a passionate culture.

"Jesus is always with you!"

A religion whose notes are painted

In the nuances of former religions

And play an overall concert,

Covered in these echoes.

A concert not only played

For the artists of Jesus,

But for any artist,

Making them dance together

In an artistic collaboration,

Creating an art work

That is painted in the colours

Of respect and tolerance.

"We all believe in the same god after all."

But the portrait lacks the nuance

Of being an atheist

And believes homosexuality

To be drawn by the pencil of Satan.

"An atheist is not able to give love

and homosexuality is a crime against God."

Bubbles

They are blown into the air

As the material visualisation

Of the hopes and dreams

Living inside an innocent head

And colouring this interior world.

But getting in contact

With the outside world,

Reality's cruel touch

Demonstrates their fragility.

They are shattered

By the ceiling of poverty

And they cannot pass

The wall of borders,

Revealing themselves as illusions

And falling to the ground

Like raindrops and tears.

But some find their way

Into the air,

Ready to be transported

Across the world

By the winds of Africa.

Night bubbles

Millions of bubbles

Are hanging in the sky,

Their stories of the wind

Wrapped into light

And illuminating the night.

They are dropping down

Into an obscure reality,

Where they are collected

By the delighted spectator

To chase the darkness away

And enlighten other bubbles' way.

"My dream is to travel the world."

"I want to have a good job and earn a lot of money, so I will be able to offer a good life to my wife and my children."

Living in a bubble

A bubble made of steel,

Transported across the world

By the speed of its wheels.

A microcosm of the privileged

Which is insensible to the wind,

And resists the sun's invitation

For a dance of destruction,

Because it's already been invited

And dances to an imported music,

Played by projects and success

And wrapped into air conditioning.

Meanwhile hopes are burnt

And dreams are buried

In the outside world,

But they remain

Unseen,

A glimpse

Of poverty

In a passing landscape,

Like forgotten ghosts.

Forgotten ghosts

A dance floor

Surrounded by walls,

And accompanied

By an exclusive orchestra,

Performing their songs

Of wealth and power,

Culminating into a crescendo

Of blindness and indifference.

But their music,

Merged into the wind,

Slips away

And reaches the ears

Of society's forgotten ghosts,

Visible only

To the eyes of those

Who choose to see.

They try to catch the rhythm,

But will never succeed,

Condemned to remain

Spectators

From the outside world.

This picture was taken at a christmas party for the children of the centre where I worked. Many of the invited authorities were late and left earlier, without making any excuses, showing obviously how little they cared, while others didn't come at all.

A song of illusions

Yowo, yowo, bonsoir!

Not a human being

Is passing by,

But the incorporation

Of a world

Of wealth and perfection,

Yowo, yowo, bonsoir!

Perceived as a reality,

Instead of only a song

Of an illusionary rhythm,

Yowo, yowo, bonsoir!

Creating an immaterial border

Between two dance floors,

Painted in different colours,

Yowo, yowo, bonsoir,

Ça va bien, merci!

But an invitation

Across the border

And an accepting hand

Are sufficient

To make us realize,

That we all belong

To the family of humanity,

Equally dancing

To the song of life.

Bonsoir ma sœur !

Comment tu vas?

Yowo=white person in Fon
Yowo, yowo, bonsoir=a song often sung to white people in the streets

Au parc national de la Pendjari

Un microcosme caché

Des griffes du monde,

Mais qui s'est mis à nu

Et qui expose ses secrets

Aux yeux mordants du soleil,

Sa source de vie

Et son pire ennemi.

Brûlés par le feu,

Les paysages sont revêtus

Par le passage des saisons

Et montrent leurs visages différents,

Marqués par les traces

De nombreux animaux.

Pour ne pas se perdre,

Il faut suivre la route

Qui invite à la découverte

De la métamorphose des paysages

Qui murmurent au vent

Leur chanson de l'infini.

« Pour ne pas se perdre, il faut suivre la route qui invite à la découverte de la métamorphose des paysages. »

La chanson de l'infini

Des fragments de pensées,

Caressés par le vent,

S'envolent avec leur amant

Vers les collines

Peintes par l'horizon

Pour se mêler à leur chanson

Et laissent derrière eux

Une âme en quête de liberté.

An ocean of memories

Foot prints in the sand,

Transient witnesses

Of memories sketched by joy,

But bound to a short existence.

Washed away by the tide

And carried by the wind

Beyond the horizon,

Where they sank down with the sun,

They are now

Rolling along with the waves

And washing clear

The sands of the horizon,

Leaving them blank,

Waiting

To be covered

By new foot prints.

Les perles de la mémoire

Le collier de l'horizon,

Enfilé par les perles de l'océan,

Peintes en turquise,

Qui se mélangent à la lumière rose

Des nuages en passage.

Un jeu de couleurs louant,

Limité que par l`horizon,

Mais restant toujours une réflexion,

Affaiblie par le temps

Et destinée à disparaître.

African sunset

The sky is slowly changing clothes,

Getting dressed in the garment of the night,

Weaved of dreams and mysteries.

But taking off the rays of the day,

It plays the last notes of its concert

In all nuances of red,

Leading the gaze

Of the attentive listener

Towards a glimpse of infinity.

Lost in eternity

Sitting at the edge

Of the world,

Let the pieces

Of our conversation

Be carried by the waves

To the horizon.

The stars will show them

The course to follow.

Let our bodies

Be dematerialized

And merged into the wind,

So we may become

One thought,

Dancing with the night

And lost in eternity.

One thought,

Dancing with the night

And lost in eternity.

The final note

The last note of the concert

Is vibrating in the air,

Still visible to the eyes

And painting the end

Of its colourful symphony.

You're trying to catch it,

But it's already fading away,

Like a breath

Bound to disappear

With the wind

And leaving a bittersweet smell.

A gift written

In immaterial ink

And submitted to transience,

Remaining nothing

But two bar lines

In time's eternal composition.

Dancing with the wind

One day,

We will whisper

The story of our friendship

To the wind,

Taking it to a dance floor,

That is not painted

In the colours of

Nationalities and social classes,

Where you are not considered

As the poor African

And I not as a Yowo,

But as equal human beings.

A dance floor painted

In a colourful music

Played by the orchestra

Of humanity,

Making us all dance

With the colours of the wind.

For all those in Benin I met as strangers, but left as friends and who added their colours to the picture of my journey.

Tableau des matières

The colours of Benin *8*

Échos musicaux *10*

A concert of languages *12*

Colonization *14*

Cultural self-doubts *16*

Artistic collaboration *18*

Bubbles *20*

Night bubbles *22*

Living in a bubble *24*

Forgotten ghosts *26*

A song of illusions *28*

Au parc national de la Pendjari *30*

La chanson de l'infini *32*

An ocean of memories *34*

Les perles de la mémoire *36*

African sunset *38*

Lost in eternity *40*

The final note *42*

Dancing with the wind *44*

Sophie MODERT was born in 1997 in Luxembourg. After receiving her higher education entrance qualification, she spent around 4 months in the Republic of Benin as part of a voluntary service. The poems as well as the pictures in this book are the artistic witnesses of this very special journey. Sophie Modert publishes her poems regularly on the literary blog *just thoughts* and has won different awards at contests like the *Jeune Printemps du Luxembourg* or the *Prix Laurence*.